THE USBORNE SOCCER SCHOOL
DEAD BALL SKILLS

Richard Dungworth
Designed by Neil Francis

Illustrations by Bob Bond • Photographs by Chris Cole
Edited by Cheryl Evans • Managing designer: Stephen Wright
Consultant: John Shiels,
Bobby Charlton International Soccer Schools Ltd.

With special thanks to soccer players Brooke Astle, David Buckley, James Peter Greatrex,
John Jackson, Sarah Leigh, Nathan Miles, Christopher Sharples, Jody Spence, Christopher White,
and to their coach, Bryn Cooper. Thanks also to John Scott, Alexander Robinson and
Susan Robinson, for their expertise and assistance with the American edition.

Library photographs: Allsport UK, Empics

DTP by John Russell

CONTENTS

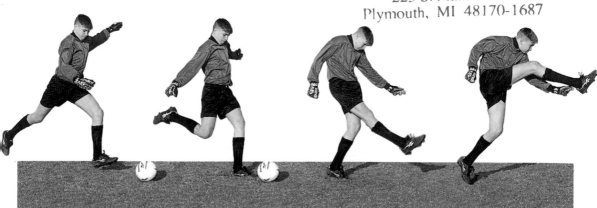

DEAD BALL BASICS

Nearly half of all goals scored in soccer come as a result of free kicks, corner kicks, throw-ins or penalties. To take full advantage of these situations, you need special soccer skills, called dead ball skills. In this book you'll find out exactly what these are, and how you and your teammates can perfect them.

This player is getting ready to take a penalty (see page 28).

WHAT IS A DEAD BALL?

Every so often in a soccer game, a player will hit the ball off the field, break one of the rules, score a goal, or suffer an injury. In each case the game stops temporarily. The ball is said to be "out of play", or "dead". To restart the game, you have to use a particular kind of kick or throw to bring the dead ball back into play.

Because a dead ball is out of play, you can use your hands to place it before you take the restart kick.

RESTART KICKS AND THROWS

If the ball goes off the field, play is restarted with a goal kick, corner kick or throw-in, depending on where the ball left the field.

If the game stops because a player has broken a soccer rule, it is restarted with a free kick or, in certain cases, a penalty kick.

Whenever a player scores a goal, or after a break in play between periods of the game, the game is restarted with a center kick.

If play is stopped for any other reason, such as injury, it is restarted with a drop ball. You'll find out more about each type of restart later on.

DEAD BALL ADVANTAGES

Here, the team in red is about to take a free kick. This typical dead ball situation shows three of the main advantages of playing the ball when it is dead, rather than when it is in normal, "open" play.

★ You have plenty of time and space. The other team's players have to stand a set distance away, and cannot interfere by tackling or obstructing you.

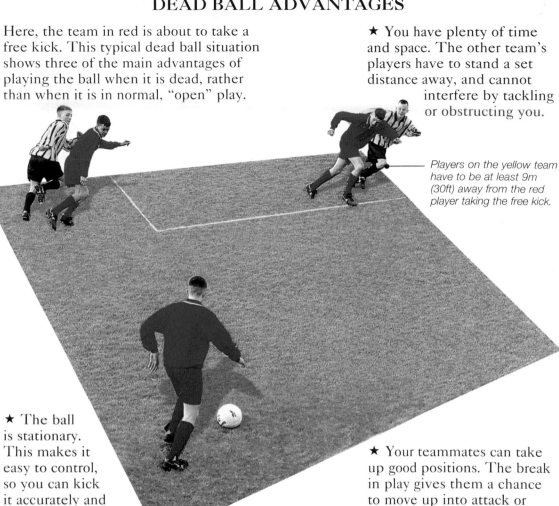

Players on the yellow team have to be at least 9m (30ft) away from the red player taking the free kick.

★ The ball is stationary. This makes it easy to control, so you can kick it accurately and confidently.

★ Your teammates can take up good positions. The break in play gives them a chance to move up into attack or drop back into defense.

USING SET PLAYS

The other major advantage of a dead ball is that it gives you a chance to use a carefully pre-planned team move, or "set play". You can rehearse various set plays in practice, and use them to outwit your opponents during a game.

Throughout this book you'll find diagrams like the one on the right. These show specific set plays for you and your teammates to try. On these diagrams, a dotted red arrow shows the path of a player and a solid blue arrow shows the path of the ball.

This set play diagram shows the free kick move that the red players are about to use in the picture above.

This player has drawn his opponent away to make space for his teammate to receive the ball.

SOCCER WORDS

To explain the techniques and tactics involved in playing a dead ball, this book uses a handful of special soccer words. These pages introduce all the technical terms that you'll come across as you read about dead ball skills. Each term is shown in **bold** type.

FINDING YOUR WAY AROUND THE FIELD

If you kick the ball toward your opponents' goal, you are playing it **upfield.** Toward you own goal is **downfield.**

The **wings** are the edges of the field along either sideline. A ball played across from either wing to the middle of the field is a **cross.**

The third of the field nearest to your own goal is your team's **defensive third.**

The middle third of the field is the **midfield.**

The third of the field nearest your opponents' goal is your team's **attacking third.**

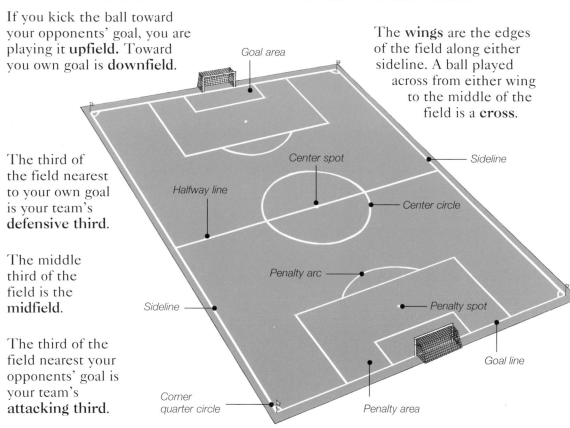

Goal area

Center spot

Sideline

Halfway line

Center circle

Penalty arc

Sideline

Penalty spot

Corner quarter circle

Penalty area

Goal line

THE REFEREE

The **referee** is an official who controls a soccer game. It is his job to decide when to stop and restart play. He uses a whistle and special arm signals (which you'll see later on in this book) to show the players his decisions.

LINESMEN

Two **linesmen** help the referee by watching the game from opposite sides of the field. Each linesman uses a flag to signal to the referee if the ball goes out of play or if he sees a player breaking any of the soccer rules.

TYPES OF PLAYERS

A soccer team is made up of a **goalkeeper**, or "goalie", who guards his team's goal, and ten **outfield** players. Each outfield player **marks** a member of the other team. This means keeping close to him to stop him from receiving or moving with the ball.

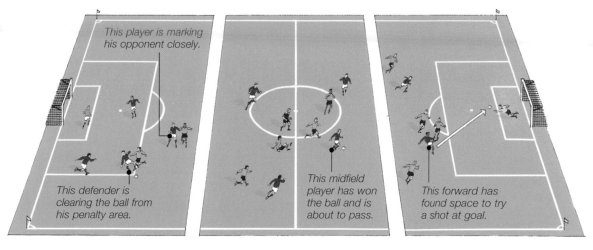

This player is marking his opponent closely.

This defender is clearing the ball from his penalty area.

This midfield player has won the ball and is about to pass.

This forward has found space to try a shot at goal.

Defenders play mostly in their defensive third. Their main job is to prevent the other team's players from having a chance to score.

Midfield players are the link between defense and attack. They move the ball upfield, and try to pass to a teammate who can score.

Forwards push upfield into the attacking third, hoping to receive a pass which will give them a chance to shoot at goal.

WHAT DOES OFFSIDES MEAN?

You are not allowed to play the ball while you are in an **offsides** position. You are offsides if you are nearer to your opponents' goal line than the ball at the moment it is passed to you, unless there are two or more opposing players at least as close to their goal line. You can't be offsides if your are within your own half of the field.

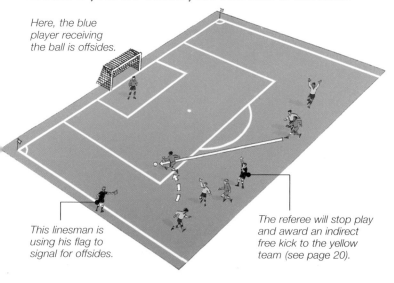

Here, the blue player receiving the ball is offsides.

This linesman is using his flag to signal for offsides.

The referee will stop play and award an indirect free kick to the yellow team (see page 20).

FOOT PARTS

Most of the skills in this book involve using one of these three different parts of your foot.

The **instep**, or **inside** of your foot, is the part from your big toe to your ankle.

The **outside** of your foot is the part from your little toe back to your ankle.

The **top**, or **laces** is the area on the upper part of your foot, covered by your shoelaces.

CENTER KICKS

The referee tosses a coin to decide which team kicks off.

Every soccer game begins with a center kick. This first dead ball opportunity, called the "kick-off", gives you an early chance to take control. Center kicks are also used to get the second half underway, to restart the game whenever a team scores a goal, and to begin any periods of extra time.

Wait for the referee to blow his whistle before you take the kick.

CENTER KICK RULES

All center kicks are taken from the center spot. When you take the kick, every player must be in his own half. Once you've kicked the ball, you mustn't kick it again until it has been touched by another player. You can't score straight from the center spot.

Opposing players must be outside the center circle when you take the kick.

You have to play the ball forward from the spot, into the other team's half.

A SHORT, SAFE CENTER KICK

A center kick gives you possession of the ball in midfield. To keep possession, so that you can control play, use a short pass to a teammate standing alongside you in the center circle.

Use your instep to tap the ball forward gently into the path of your teammate.

Make sure the ball crosses the halfway line completely.

Your teammate can quickly pass the ball to one of your team's players who has space to receive it without being challenged.

PRESSURING YOUR OPPONENTS

STAR CENTER

You can use a longer center kick to move play upfield quickly and put pressure on the other team.

Kick the ball upfield into the attacking third. Aim for a space behind the other team's midfield players.

Your forwards should sprint upfield from the halfway line to challenge for possession.

This tactic might well cause your team to lose the ball, but it can sometimes create an early scoring chance.

Here, the Croatian players Alen Boksic and Davor Suker talk tactics as they prepare to take a center kick. Unless their team is trailing in the late stages of a game, they will probably opt for a short center kick to make sure that their team keeps possession of the ball.

CREATING AN OVERLOAD

If you decide to try a long center kick, your team will have a better chance of winning the ball if several of your players gather on one side of the field.

Angle your kick to the "overloaded" side of the field, into the path of your forwards.

The other team may realize what you are planning, and move across to the overloaded side of the field.

In this case, try switching your center kick move at the last minute, playing the ball to the other side.

THROW-IN TECHNIQUE

If an opposing player knocks the ball over either sideline, one of your team's players has to throw it back onto the field. This is known as taking a throw-in. It is the only type of restart which involves using your hands to bring a dead ball back into play.

A linesman points his flag like this to signal a throw-in.

The team playing in the direction of the flag takes the throw.

THROW-IN RULES

To throw the ball back into play you have to bring it forward from behind your head, using both hands. As you release the ball, part of both your feet must be touching the ground, on or behind the sideline.

  You cannot score a goal by throwing the ball straight into your opponents' goal.

Feet on ground, on or behind sideline.

HOW TO HOLD THE BALL

Make sure that you hold the ball with your fingers spread around its back and sides. Your thumbs should nearly touch.

Holding the ball like this lets you control it more easily as you release your throw.

PRACTICING YOUR THROW-IN

You need to be able to throw accurately or you may give away the ball. To improve your throw, try this exercise with a partner.

Stand about 10m (33ft) apart. Use throw-ins to pass the ball back and forth. Throw the ball to your partner's feet so that he can control it easily.

As you get better at throwing the ball, your partner can give you a specific target area. Try throwing to your partner's head, chest and thigh.

TAKING A LONGER THROW-IN

Most professional soccer teams have at least one player who specializes in throwing the ball a long way. Practice the technique shown here to develop a long, accurate throw-in.

At least part of your trailing foot must be touching the ground.

Place your leading foot close behind the sideline.

Arch your back to bring the ball as far back as possible.

Use your hands and fingers to direct the ball's flight.

Leading leg

Hold the ball in front of your head and take a couple of quick steps toward the sideline.

Take a long final stride to reach the line, bringing the ball back behind your head.

With the weight on your leading leg, whip the upper part of your body forward to catapult the ball away.

THROWING AWAY POSSESSION

If you break one of the rules when you take a throw-in, the referee will ask the other team to retake the throw. Be careful not to lose possession with a foul throw. The pictures below show the things you need to avoid to keep your throw-in legal.

FOUL THROW - The player's feet are too far over the sideline for a legal throw-in.

FOUL THROW - The thrower's right foot is off the ground as he releases the ball.

FOUL THROW - The player hasn't brought the ball far enough back over his head.

STAR THROW

Here, Gary Neville, playing for Manchester United, prepares to launch a long throw-in along the wing.

THROW-IN TACTICS

A throw-in is more than just a way of bringing the ball back onto the field. A good throw can start an attacking move, or ease the pressure on your defense. You and your teammates can use the tactics introduced here to make the most of throw-in moves during a game.

THROW-IN TIPS

Always try to throw to a teammate who can receive the ball without being challenged. Whenever possible, and especially in your own half, send the ball upfield.

Several of your players should move into throwing range to increase your choice of receiver.

As you prepare to throw, your teammates need to find open space by moving away from marking players.

A throw into an open space, for a teammate to run onto, is often more effective than one aimed directly at him.

You can even throw over a teammate into open space behind him, so that he can turn and chase the ball.

You can often catch the other team off guard if the member of your team nearest to the ball when it goes out of play takes the throw-in quickly. However quickly you throw, make sure you bring the ball back over your head.

A DECOY MOVE

As you prepare to throw, your teammates can use a decoy move like this to create space for a particular player to receive the ball.

1. Player A starts an angled run as though to receive the throw, drawing his marking player away with him.

2. Player B, running in from the opposite angle, moves into the space created by Player A's "decoy run".

3. The thrower delivers his throw into the path of player B, who can receive the ball unchallenged and push upfield into attack.

USING A WALL PASS THROW-IN

Once you've taken a throw, get right back into play. By using one of your team-mates as a "wall" to knock your throw back to you, you can rejoin the action immediately. This wall pass move is particularly useful if all your players are closely marked.

1. Throw to a nearby team-mate's feet, so that he can control the ball easily.

Move forward onto the field.

2. The receiver uses his instep to hit a first touch pass back to you.

3. You can build on this basic wall pass move by playing the ball upfield for the player who first received your throw to run onto.

Here, the player who took the throw is about to use his instep to pass the ball upfield into the path of his teammate.

This opposing player is moving across to challenge for the ball.

As his marking player moves away, the player who originally acted as the "wall" turns to run into open space and receive his teammate's pass.

THROWING INTO THE PENALTY AREA

If your team is awarded a throw-in within the attacking third, try using a long throw into the penalty area. Your teammates can't be offside from a throw-in, so they can move upfield to threaten your opponents' goal.

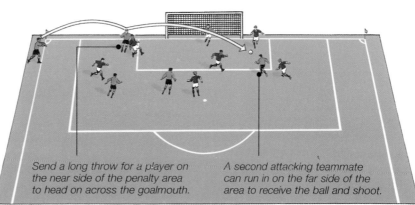

Send a long throw for a player on the near side of the penalty area to head on across the goalmouth.

A second attacking teammate can run in on the far side of the area to receive the ball and shoot.

GOAL KICKS

If a player on the other team knocks the ball out of play over your goal line, a member of your team has to restart the game with a goal kick. Like center kicks, goal kicks give you a chance either to control possession of the ball or move play upfield quickly.

The referee will point at the goal area to signal a goal kick.

GOAL KICK RULES

To bring the ball back into play with a goal kick, you have to kick it from within your goal area, so that it leaves the penalty area. You can't kick the ball again until another player has touched it.

A team's goalkeeper usually takes its goal kicks.

Goal area

Penalty area

Opposing players must be outside the penalty area when the goal kick is taken.

The ball must be stationary when you kick it.

Notice how this player is leaning back to give his kick lift, and taking a high backswing for maximum power.

THE OUTFIELD KICKER OPTION

If your goalkeeper makes a bad goal kick, an opposing player may intercept the ball and shoot while your goalie is out of position. You may prefer one of your outfield players to take the kick, so that your goalkeeper can stay in position.

There is a drawback to an outfield player taking a goal kick. It makes it harder for your defenders to catch opposing players offsides (see page 5) after the kick. The kicker should rush forward to get level with his teammates as quickly as he can.

TAKING A LONG GOAL KICK

You can use a long goal kick to move play out of your team's defensive third. Use the kicking technique shown here to send the ball as far upfield as you can. By hitting the ball below its midline, you can make it rise and travel over players.

Lift your kicking foot in a high backswing.

Lean back slightly as you kick.

Use your arms for balance.

Take a short run up, from a slight angle, so that you can strike the ball with force.

With a long last stride, get your nonkicking foot slightly behind and to the side of the ball.

Swing your kicking foot forward to strike the lower half of the ball with your laces.

Follow through with your kicking leg to power the ball as far upfield as possible.

AIMING

Try to pick out a teammate with your long goal kick, or at least aim it where there are enough of your players to stand a good chance of winning the ball. Here Dino Baggio (Italy) and John Sheridan (Republic of Ireland) challenge for a long goal kick ball.

USING A SHORTER GOAL KICK

You can make sure that your team keeps possession of the ball by sending a shorter goal kick to an unmarked teammate near your own penalty area. Be careful to deliver the ball so that it is easy to control. Some of your midfield players can drop back into your defensive third so that at least one of your teammates is free to receive the ball safely.

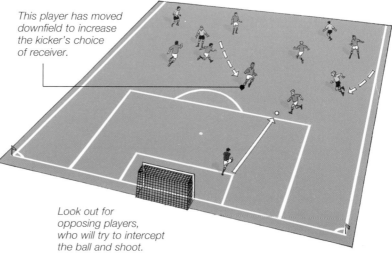

This player has moved downfield to increase the kicker's choice of receiver.

Look out for opposing players, who will try to intercept the ball and shoot.

CORNER KICKS

When a defending player hits the ball over his own goal line, the referee awards the attacking team a corner kick. This gives you a chance to play the ball across your opponents' goalmouth for a teammate to shoot at goal.

To signal a corner, the referee points to the corner flag.

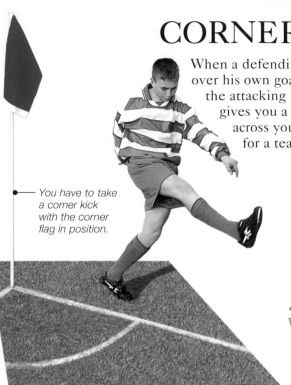
You have to take a corner kick with the corner flag in position.

CORNER KICK RULES

To take a corner, you kick the ball from within the corner quarter circle nearest to the point where it went out of play.

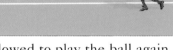
Members of the other team must be at least 9m (30ft) from the ball.

You're not allowed to play the ball again until another player has touched it.

PLACING THE BALL FOR A CORNER KICK

You need to place the ball in the corner circle in such a way that you can kick it without the flag blocking your run up or swing. The best place to put the ball will depend on whether you are left- or right-footed.

Here, the ball is placed correctly for a left-footed corner kicker.

Here, the ball is placed correctly for a right-footed corner kicker.

CROSSING FROM THE CORNER

If you hit a long, lofted corner kick to a teammate just beyond the far side of the goal, he'll have a chance to shoot from behind the goalkeeper's view.

A player who receives a corner kick can't be offsides, so your teammates can move up toward the goalmouth to receive your corner cross.

INSWINGERS

You can make your cross even more effective by bending it, so that the ball swings in toward the goal. A corner kick like this is known as an inswinger.

HOW DO YOU BEND A CORNER KICK?

The secret to bending a corner kick cross is to strike the ball off-center so that it spins as it travels through the air. The easiest way to do this is to use the instep of your kicking foot to strike the outside edge of the ball. This right-footed player is about to hit an inswinger from the left corner in this way.

You also need to remember to hit the ball below its midline, so that your cross has plenty of lift.

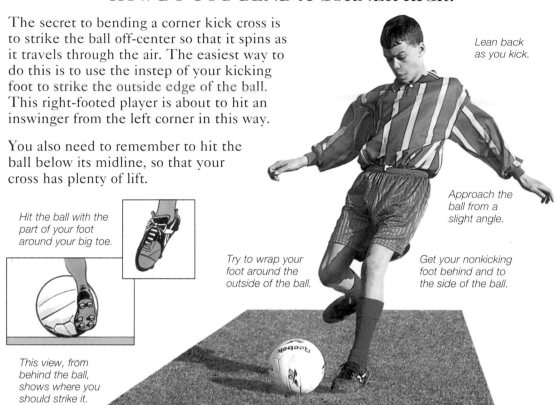

Lean back as you kick.

Approach the ball from a slight angle.

Hit the ball with the part of your foot around your big toe.

Try to wrap your foot around the outside of the ball.

Get your nonkicking foot behind and to the side of the ball.

This view, from behind the ball, shows where you should strike it.

PRACTICING YOUR CROSS

As you get better at judging the distance, see how much you can bend each cross.

Practice this with a partner to get used to the length and height of a good cross. Stand on the front corners of the penalty area - or about 40m (130ft) apart if you're not on a field. This is about the distance from the corner to the farthest post. Hit crosses to one another, trying to deliver the ball so that your partner can catch it just above his head.

WHO KICKS?

Bending a kick using your instep makes the ball swing away to the left if you're right-footed, or to the right if you're left-footed. Make sure that you pick the correct player to take an inswinger from a particular side of the field.

A right-footed player takes inswingers from left of the goal.

A left-footed player takes inswingers from right of the goal.

CORNER KICK MOVES

A cross from the corner is an example of a "fifty-fifty" ball - both teams have an equal chance of gaining possession. You can tip the balance in your team's favor by using a preplanned corner move. These pages suggest several corner kick set plays for you to try.

FINDING SPACE TO RECEIVE A CROSS

For any corner kick move to be successful, one of your teammates in the penalty area needs to be free to receive the ball and shoot. As you prepare to take a corner, your forwards should try to move away from their marking players to find space.

Here, the blue forwards are getting ready to receive a cross from the right-hand corner.

The blue players in the far side of the penalty area can strike from a long cross or a flicked-on ball (see below).

This blue player is trying to find space to receive a shorter, driven cross (see page 18).

There is a good chance for a shot into this side of the goal, which the red team has left unguarded.

A FLICK-ON FROM THE NEAR POST

For this move, one of your teammates needs to move into space around the goalpost nearest to the corner that you are kicking from. Send a short, inswinging cross to this player at the near post.

The player receiving the corner cross uses his head to flick the ball on across the goal. One of your other forwards runs in on the far side of the goal area to receive the flicked-on ball and shoot.

Judge your cross so that your teammate can head the ball.

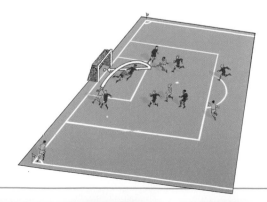

LAYING THE BALL BACK

This alternative near post move can be as effective as a flick-on across the goal. Send a cross to a teammate at the near post. Instead of heading the ball across the goalmouth, the receiver "lays it back".

This means heading it down into the path of a teammate running in from midfield.

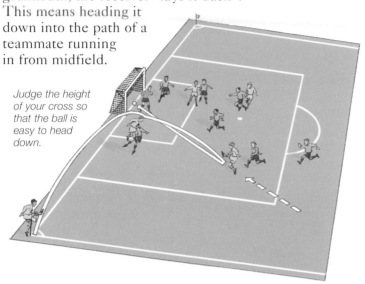

Judge the height of your cross so that the ball is easy to head down.

OUTSWINGING CORNERS

Another option is to bend your corner kick cross away from the goalmouth. This kind of corner is called an "outswinger". It makes it easier for your teammates moving toward goal to head the ball well.

Players can run onto your cross from the edge of the penalty area.

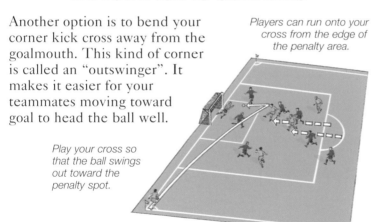

Play your cross so that the ball swings out toward the penalty spot.

By moving out toward the corner, or over toward the far post, your teammates can draw defenders away from the near side of the penalty area. This creates space for a player to run onto a shorter outswinging cross.

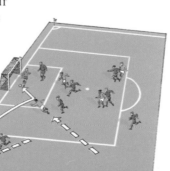

This player is drawing away his marking player to create space.

CORNER ACTION

Try to spot different corner moves when you watch professional players in action. Here, the left-footed corner taker has hit an inswinging corner cross. His teammates in the goal area will try to head the ball down into the goal.

WHO KICKS?

As with inswingers (see page 15), you need to pick the correct kicker to take an outswinging corner from a particular side of the field.

A right-footed player takes outswinging corners from the right-hand side of the goal.

A left-footed player takes outswinging corners from the left-hand side of the goal.

SHORT AND DRIVEN CORNERS

Because a swinging cross is the most popular corner kick option, it is also the most predictable. To keep the other team guessing, vary your corner kick tactics every now and then. You can use a driven corner for a faster-paced cross, or a short corner for an attack from a different angle.

TAKING A DRIVEN CORNER

When you hit a swinging, lofted cross, the ball takes a long time to reach the goal area because it follows a curved path through the air. By striking a low, straight, powerful cross, you can send the ball across the goalmouth more quickly.

As you run up, get your nonkicking foot up alongside the ball. Don't lean back. Keep your body upright and over the ball.

With your knee over the ball, and your toes pointing down, strike the ball just below its center with the top of your foot.

Follow through with your kicking leg to power the ball across into the penalty area. It will travel in a straight line, rising slightly.

DRIVEN CORNER MOVES

Try to send a driven corner either to a player on the near side of the goal area, or one around the middle of the penalty area. A driven cross will stay low, so the receiver must be prepared to kick a waist-high volley, or even try a diving header. Your other teammates can create space for him by moving as though to receive a longer cross (see page 14) or a short corner (see page 19).

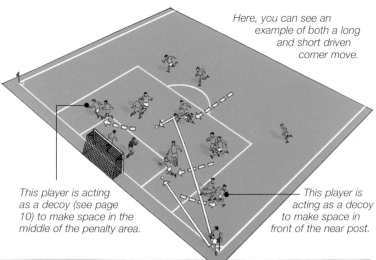

Here, you can see an example of both a long and short driven corner move.

This player is acting as a decoy (see page 10) to make space in the middle of the penalty area.

This player is acting as a decoy to make space in front of the near post.

PLAYING A SHORT CORNER

You can use this simple pass and return tactic, or "short corner", to build up an attacking move from the corner of the pitch.

One of your teammates moves within easy passing range of the corner. Send the ball along the ground to this nearby player.

As soon as you have taken the kick, run into open space downfield from your teammate, so that he can pass the ball back to you.

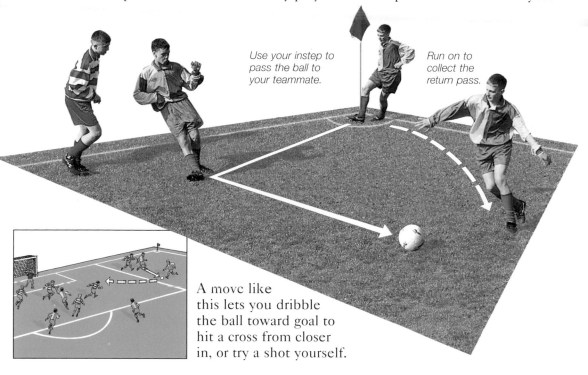

Use your instep to pass the ball to your teammate.

Run on to collect the return pass.

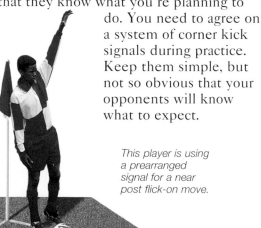

A move like this lets you dribble the ball toward goal to hit a cross from closer in, or try a shot yourself.

SIGNALING THE MOVE

When you've decided what kind of corner move to use, signal to your teammates so that they know what you're planning to do. You need to agree on a system of corner kick signals during practice. Keep them simple, but not so obvious that your opponents will know what to expect.

This player is using a prearranged signal for a near post flick-on move.

CORNER SKILLS GAME

Mark out a special field, 40m (130ft) wide but only about 15m (50ft) long. Play a game of five- or seven-a-side within this area. The short, wide field means that most of the action takes place around either goalmouth. This gives you lots of chances to try out different corner moves.

Restart play with a corner, wherever the ball goes off the field.

Goal

Goal

FREE KICK BASICS

If one of your opponents "commits an offense" by breaking a soccer rule, the referee will stop the game and ask your team to restart play with a free kick. There are two types of free kicks – direct, to punish serious offenses, and indirect for less serious ones.

To signal an indirect free kick, the referee raises his arm.

SERIOUS OFFENSES

The referee will award a direct free kick if a player kicks, trips, charges, strikes, pushes, holds or jumps at an opponent; if an outfield player deliberately uses his hands to control the ball, or if a goalkeeper handles the ball outside his penalty area.

If a player commits a direct free kick offense like this in his own penalty area, the referee will award the other team a penalty kick (see page 28).

Here, the player in yellow is holding his opponent back, rather than playing the ball. An unfair challenge like this is known as a foul.

INDIRECT FREE KICK OFFENSES

These pictures show the various offenses for which a referee will award an indirect free kick. The three types of offenses illustrated on the top row are specifically for goalkeepers.

Time-wasting by holding the ball for a long time.

Using hands to receive a backpass from a teammate.

Taking more than four steps while holding the ball.

Charging or obstructing the opposing goalkeeper.

Playing dangerously (here, kicking a high ball).

Charging or obstructing a player who isn't on the ball.

Receiving the ball while in an offsides position (see page 5).

FREE KICK RULES

To take a free kick, you kick the ball from the point on the field where the offense took place. The ball must be stationary when you kick it, and the other team's players have to be at least 9m (30ft) away. You can't play the ball again until it has been touched by another player.

If the free kick is direct, you are allowed to score straight from the kick.

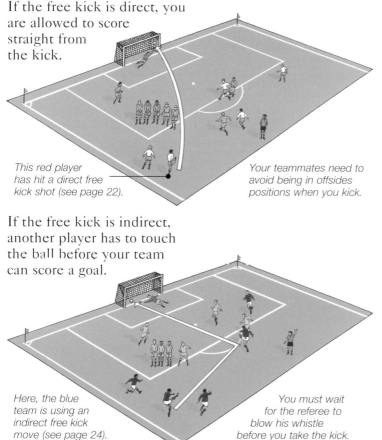

This red player has hit a direct free kick shot (see page 22).

Your teammates need to avoid being in offsides positions when you kick.

If the free kick is indirect, another player has to touch the ball before your team can score a goal.

Here, the blue team is using an indirect free kick move (see page 24).

You must wait for the referee to blow his whistle before you take the kick.

SPECIAL CASES

If you are awarded a free kick in your own penalty area, you have to kick the ball out of the penalty area to bring it back into play.

Opposing players must be outside the penalty area when you kick.

If the kick is inside your goal area, you can take it from any part of that area.

If you are given an indirect free kick inside your opponent's goal area, you take the kick from the edge of the goal area.

Your opponents are allowed to stand on their goal line, between the posts, despite being less than 9m (30ft) away.

TAKING A FREE KICK IN YOUR OWN HALF

The top priority when you take a free kick in your own half of the field is to make sure that your team keeps the ball. Use a simple pass to a player in open space.

Aim your kick away from any nearby opponent hoping to steal the ball.

Send the ball upfield whenever possible.

DIRECT FREE KICKS

A free kick in the attacking third gives you a good chance to score a spectacular goal. You're most likely to score if you keep your free kick move simple. These pages look at the simplest of all attacking free kicks – a direct shot at goal from the edge of the penalty area.

THE DEFENSIVE WALL

When you take a free kick near the penalty area, your opponents will usually protect their goalmouth by forming a defensive wall. Several players will stand side by side to block your shooting line. To score, you need to get the ball past this wall of players.

The players in the wall will try to block one side of the goalmouth, while their goalkeeper guards the other.

BENDING YOUR SHOT AROUND THE WALL

By striking the outside edge of the ball with your instep, you can bend a free kick so that it swings away to your nonkicking side. Don't hit the ball too low down or it will rise over the goal.

To bend a kick in the other direction, so that it swings out to your kicking side, use the outside of your foot to strike the inside edge of the ball. Keep the toes of your kicking foot pointed down as you kick.

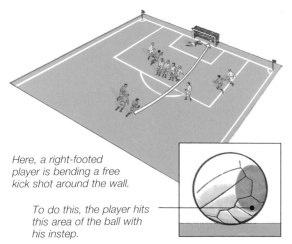

Here, a right-footed player is bending a free kick shot around the wall.

To do this, the player hits this area of the ball with his instep.

Here, a right-footed player is bending a shot in the other direction.

To do this, the player hits this area of the ball with the outside of his foot.

BENDING SHOT PRACTICE

To practice your swerving shot, put one corner flag in the center of the goal, and another on the penalty spot. Place the ball on the penalty arc, in line with the flags. Try to bend a kick around one side of the nearest flag into the other side of the goalmouth.

Try bending shots in either direction.

Try placing the ball farther around the arc so that you have to bend your kick more.

SHOOTING STAR

Here, Roberto Baggio is powering a bending free kick shot at goal. One of his Juventus teammates helps to shield the move until the last moment.

USING A FAKE CROSSOVER

You can use this tactic to disguise the direction of a direct free kick shot.

1. You and a teammate (ideally a player who kicks with the opposite foot to you) both prepare as though to take the kick.

2. Your teammate runs up to the ball, as though to shoot, but steps over it at the last minute.

Your teammate's run will help to hide your shot.

3. Time your own run up so that just after your teammate fakes a shot, you hit a powerful shot at goal. Your teammate can continue his run to follow in your shot.

FREE KICK MOVES

Even if you can hit a hard, swerving shot, you are unlikely to score from a free kick unless you can create an element of surprise. You need to leave your opponents unsure which direction your attack will come from. Use one of the moves described here to baffle the defense.

STRETCHING THE WALL

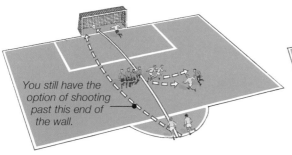

You still have the option of shooting past this end of the wall.

One or two of your teammates join the end of the defensive wall, to block the goalkeeper's view of the free kick.

As you take the kick, your players in the wall break away to let your shot past, turning to follow it in.

MAKING YOUR OWN WALL

Two or three of your teammates form a separate wall a few feet in front of the ball to hide the kick from view.

Your players move off as you kick. They need to hide the ball as long as possible, without getting in its way.

CREATING A GAP IN THE WALL

This move requires split-second timing. One or two of your forwards try to squeeze right up in front of the middle of the defensive wall. By moving away from the wall as you shoot, they may be able to create a gap for your shot to pass through.

Your players musn't move off too soon or the wall will close up.

INDIRECT MOVES

From an indirect free kick you have to pass the ball before a player can shoot. A simple pass to one side lets you quickly change the angle of your attack so that one of your teammates can have a clear shot at goal.

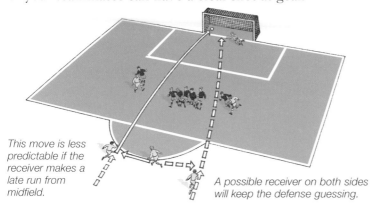

This move is less predictable if the receiver makes a late run from midfield.

A possible receiver on both sides will keep the defense guessing.

THE BACK PASS SWITCH

You can try this move to switch the direction of an indirect free kick attack. Approach the ball as though to kick to a teammate on one side. Instead, roll the ball backward to a player on the other side to shoot.

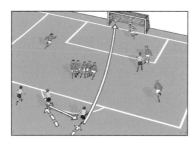

Use the underside of your foot to roll the ball to a teammate behind you.

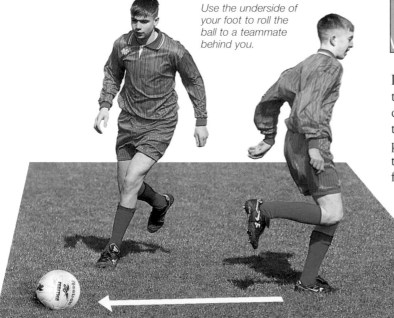

TWO-PASS MOVES

Using two passes in a free kick move lets you move the ball to one side of the wall and closer to the goal, for a good shooting position. Try this basic two-pass move.

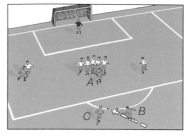

Player A takes up a position slightly downfield from the wall, facing back toward the ball. Left-footed player B and right-footed player C both prepare as though to take the free kick.

Player B does a fake over the ball, running on diagonally to one side of the wall. As he does so, player C sends a pass along the ground to player A in front of the wall. He in turn passes the ball sideways for player B to run onto and shoot at goal.

MORE FREE KICK MOVES

You need to prepare suitable moves for free kicks from different positions in the attacking third. On these pages you can see some suggested moves for free kicks near either wing. You can also find out how you and your teammates can perfect your own free kick moves.

FREE KICKS FROM THE WING

When your team is awarded a free kick at either side of your opponent's penalty area, the other team's players will usually move out to be level with their defensive wall. This stops your teammates from taking up positions near the goal, where they would be offsides.

In a free kick situation like this, you can attack by crossing the ball into space behind the defense, for your teammates to run onto.

Here, the blue player taking the free kick has hit a long, outswinging cross from the wing.

Each forward times his run so as to avoid being offsides.

DISGUISING A FREE KICK CROSS

Try using this set play to disguise a free kick cross to the near post.

1. Player A, a left-footer, runs in as if to take the free kick. At the same time, players C and D move off as if to receive a long, outswinging cross to the far post.

2. Player A does a fake over the ball. His right-footed teammate, player B, runs in to hit a short, inswinging cross into the space created by decoys C and D. Players E and F run onto the ball to shoot.

USING THE WING

A cross from a free kick at the side of the penalty area is fairly predictable. You may be able to surprise your opponents by using a move along the wing. Send the ball toward the sideline, into the path of a player making a run from midfield.

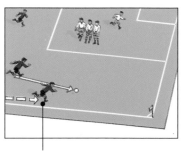

The receiver can dribble the ball upfield along the wing and send a cross into the goal area.

PRACTICING YOUR OWN FREE KICK MOVES

You can try out some of your own set plays for attacking free kicks by having a free kick competition. Split into two teams of seven or eight players. Each team takes one direct and one indirect free kick from each of five different positions outside the penalty area, while the other team defends the goal. The team which scores the most goals from their ten free kick attempts wins.

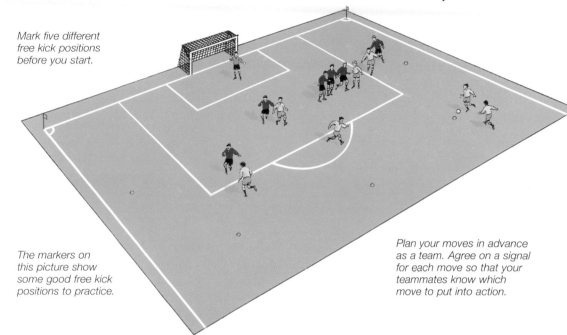

Mark five different free kick positions before you start.

The markers on this picture show some good free kick positions to practice.

Plan your moves in advance as a team. Agree on a signal for each move so that your teammates know which move to put into action.

★ Always take into consideration whether the kick is direct or indirect, and what position it is from.

★ Keep your free kick moves fairly simple. Ideally they should involve no more than three touches.

★ Remember that you cannot use any move that involves a teammate being in an offsides position.

VARYING YOUR CHOICE OF MOVE

Whichever attacking free kick move you use, it is unlikely to work if your opponents can tell what you're planning from the position of your players. Try to vary which move you use from each position. As an example, the pictures below show three very different moves involving a teammate positioned at one end of the defensive wall.

By breaking away from the wall, the forward has here distracted attention from his teammate's direct shot.

Here, the forward has moved out from the wall to take part in an indirect two-pass move (see page 25).

In this case, the player on the end of the wall has turned to run onto a ball chipped over the top of the wall.

PENALTIES

When a player commits a serious offense inside his own penalty area, the referee awards the attacking team a penalty kick. A penalty is a high-pressure, "one-on-one" situation in which you try to beat your opponents' goalkeeper with a direct shot at goal.

To signal a penalty, the referee points at the penalty spot.

Place the ball yourself, so that you know it is on a sound surface.

PENALTY RULES

To take a penalty, you shoot at goal from the penalty spot. You can't play the ball again until it has been touched by another player.

The goalkeeper can't move until you play the ball.

All other players must be outside the penalty area, beyond the arc, and downfield from the spot.

STAYING COOL

When you take a penalty, don't be indecisive or hesitant. Pick your target area and concentrate on hitting a hard, low shot into that part of the goal.

A firmly hit shot just inside either post will be extremely hard to stop.

SHOOTING WITH POWER

1. The key to a low, hard shot is to keep your body over the ball as you kick, rather than leaning back.

2. Get your nonkicking foot alongside the ball so that the knee of your kicking leg is over the ball.

3. With your toes pointing down, use the top of your kicking foot to drive the ball forward.

Use your arms for balance.

Follow through with your kicking leg for maximum power.

Kick the ball through its midline, so that it stays low.

SOFT OPTION

You may find it easier to place your penalty kick shot accurately by hitting the ball with slightly less power, using your instep.

FOLLOWING UP THE PENALTY

Your teammates should be ready to close in on the goalmouth as soon as you've taken your penalty kick.

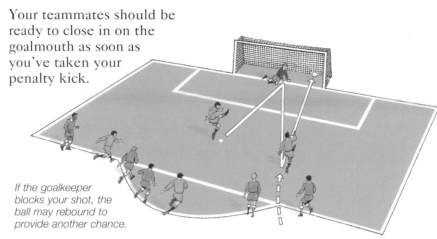

If the goalkeeper blocks your shot, the ball may rebound to provide another chance.

THE PENALTY SHOOT-OUT

If the scores are tied at the end of overtime, the teams often have a penalty competition to decide which team wins the match. This is known as a penalty "shoot-out". If one team has scored more goals after both teams have had five penalty attempts, then that team wins the match. Otherwise, the shoot-out continues until one team's penalty score passes the other team's from the same number of attempts.

These players are using a practice penalty shoot-out in training to perfect their penalty skills.

In a shoot-out, each penalty shot has to be taken by a different player, so every member of your team needs to practice.

A practice shoot-out will also improve your goalkeeper's skills.

WINNING A DROP BALL

This page introduces the least common soccer restart, called a drop ball. This is a one-on-one challenge in which a member of each team competes for possession of the ball. To win a drop ball you'll need total concentration and sharp reactions.

DROP BALL BASICS

The referee uses a drop ball to restart play after any stoppage for which neither team is responsible, such as a break in play caused by injury. Unlike other restarts, a drop ball is meant to give both teams an equal chance of gaining possession of the ball.

Two players, one from each team, face one another at the point where the ball was last in play. The referee brings the ball back into play by dropping it onto the field between them. Neither player is allowed to play the ball before it hits the ground.

If your opponents had the ball when the game was interrupted by injury, it is good sportsmanship to let them win it back from the drop ball restart deliberately.

Concentrate on the ball. Try to get your foot to it as soon as it lands.

WINNING WAYS

The simplest approach to a drop ball is to use your instep to tap the ball to a teammate on your nonkicking side.

If you think your opponent will block an instep pass, try using the outside of your foot to hook the ball away to the other side.

You can even try pushing the ball forward through the gap between your opponent's legs. Dodge past him to collect the ball.

CREATING CHANCES

The skills in this book will enable you and your team-mates to turn throw-ins, corners, free kicks and penalties into goals. To create as many opportunities as possible to use these skills during a game, you need to put pressure on your opponents so that they send the ball out of play.

PRESSURE PASSING

SHOOTING

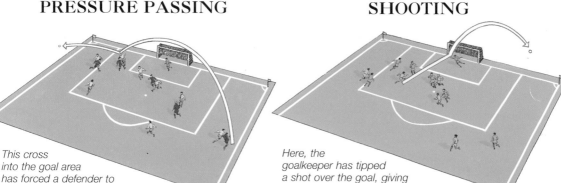

This cross into the goal area has forced a defender to head the ball out of play.

Here, the goalkeeper has tipped a shot over the goal, giving his opponents a corner kick.

You can often win a throw-in or corner by passing the ball into a space near your opponents' goal, for a teammate to chase. Your opponents will be forced to clear the ball, rather than allow you a shot at goal.

Even if you don't score, taking a shot at goal can create a second scoring chance. By blocking your shot, a defender or goalkeeper will often knock the ball out of play to give your team a corner kick.

DRIBBLING INTO ATTACK

STAR PHOTO

Here, the red player's attacking run gains his team a corner kick.

By dribbling into the other team's penalty area, or upfield along either wing, you will often force a defender to try a desperate tackle. In doing so, he may clear the ball for a throw-in or corner, or even give your team a free kick or penalty.

CHALLENGING DEFENDERS

By closing in on a defender, you can force him to play the ball in a hurry.

If one of the other team's players has possession of the ball in his defensive third, move in to challenge him. Under pressure, he is likely to send the ball out of play. This would give your team possession in a good attacking position.

Here, by attacking along the wing, Emmanuel Amunike (Nigeria) forces a defender to clear the ball for a throw-in.

INDEX

First published in 1996 by Usborne Publishing Ltd, 83-85 Saffron Hill,
London EC1N 8RT, England. Copyright © 1996 Usborne Publishing Ltd.
The name Usborne and the device ♕ are Trade Marks of Usborne Publishing Ltd.
All rights reserved. No part of this publication may be reproduced, stored in a
retrieval system or transmitted in any form or by any means, electronic,
mechanical, photocopying, recording or otherwise, without the prior
permission of the publisher. Printed in Belgium.
AE. First published in America in March 1997.

THE USBORNE
SOCCER SCHOOL